Animal Peculiarity Volume 2 Part 6

By T.P Just

~~~

Copyright © 2012 by T.P Just. All rights reserved.

I0413401

Get All The Books In The Series:

Animal Peculiarity Volume 1 [1-8]
Animal Peculiarity Volume 2 [1-8]
Just Enterprises

Table of Contents

1. Introduction

Suicide is commended as an escape from the ills of life, and riches are to be despised. Aelian's Stoicism hardly goes below the surface. His primary object is to entertain and while so doing to convey instruction in the most agreeable form.
He was among the first to break away from the age-long tradition of the periodic structure of sentences, at least for works of a serious nature, and to affect a simpler prose of short, coordinated, sometimes paratactic, clauses.
In this and in the rich variety of topics and in a certain fondness for piquant, not to say earthy, stories from the life of men and of animals one may trace the influence of the Milesian Tales.
Unfettered by any canons of style or language, picaresque, and sometimes gross, they pandered to popular taste. To adopt their technique while refining the style and imparting a moral flavour to his narratives may well have seemed to Aelian a sure way of gaining a like popularity with educated readers.
Some might find fault with his random and piece-meal handling of his theme-of that he is well aware, and in the Epilogue he defends himself with the plea that a frequent change of topic helps to maintain the reader's interest and saves him from boredom.
But as to the permanent value of his work he has no misgivings, and since. Philostratus informs us that his writings were much admired, we may assume that they appealed to cultivated circles in a way that the voluminous and possibly arid compilations of grammarians did not.

2. Fox and Hedgehog

The Fox is a rascally creature; hence poets are fond of calling it 'crafty.' The Hedgehog also is a rascal, for directly it sees the Fox approaching it rolls itself into a ball and lies still. And the Fox, unable to open his jaws and bite it, makes Water into its mouth.

And the Hedgehog is suffocated because its breathing is stopped through its being rolled up and because of the aforesaid stream. Moreover the Fox having thus tricked the Hedgehog, one scoundrel tricking another, catches it out. I have earlier described another method of capture.

3. Cows of Susa

I have ascertained that the Cows in Susa are not unacquainted even with arithmetic. And that this is no idle boast the following story bears witness. In Susa the King has a large number of Cows of which each one draws one hundred buckets (daily) to water the drier places in his parks.
Now they perform with the utmost zest the task which has either been heaped upon them or to which they have long been accustomed, and you would never see one of them idling. If however you were to urge them to draw so much as one bucketful in excess of the century, you will neither persuade nor compel them, whether by blows or by soft words, to do so. This is what Ctesias says.

The 'monops'

There is an animal in Paeonia called Monops, and it is the size of a shaggy bull. Now when this creature is pursued, in its agitation it voids fiery and acrid dung, so I am told; and should this happen to fall on any of the hunters, it kills him.

4. A home for aged Elephants

At the foot of Atlas (this mountain is celebrated by historians and also by poets) there are marvelous pasture-lands and forests of the deepest, whose dense foliage is like that of groves all shady and overarched. And that, you know, is where Elephants are said to resort in old age when heavy with years.

And Nature leads them as it were to a colony, giving them rest at last and providing them with a desired anchorage and harbor, so to speak, where they can live out the rest of their life. And they have a spring of drinking-water pure and welling up abundantly; and they are regarded as sacred and are allowed to go unmolested; and they have an agreement with the barbarians in those parts that they shall not be hunted; and it is commonly said that they are under the care of certain gods of the district who are lords of wood and valley.

And there is a story current about them, as follows. A certain King of that country was eager to kill some of them on account of the splendor and size of their tusks, in order to obtain a choice possession, for with the multitude of years and the lengthening of time these weapons of these creatures become enormous.

So when this desire came upon him he dispatched three hundred picked men to shoot this sacred herd. And all equipped they accomplished their journey with the utmost speed, and were actually nearing the spot when a pestilence suddenly seized them and laid them low: all died save only one, and he returned and rendered to him who had sent them a full account of the truly lamentable disaster. By this means it was discovered that the Elephants were beloved of the gods.

5. The Bull, its docility

The Bull, it seems that a special characteristic of the Bull is its docility, once it has been tamed and from being savage become gentle. At any rate Bulls remain quiet when harnessed to 'litters, or if you want them to lie still on their back or with their head on the ground or to sink down on their knees and carry a boy or a girl on their neck.

And you will even see a Bull bearing a woman on its back or standing erect on its hind legs while it supports with ease the entire weight of its body on some object or other. And I have even seen men dancing on the backs of Bulls, and the same men motionless there also and standing undislodged.

6. The 'Catoblepon' or Gnu

Libya is the parent of a great number and a great variety of wild animals, and moreover it seems that the same country produces the animal called the Katoblepon (down-looking). In appearance it is about the size of a bull, but it has a more grim expression, for its eyebrows are high and shaggy, and the eyes beneath are not large like those of oxen but narrower and bloodshot.

And they do not look straight ahead but down on to the ground: that is why it is called down-looking.' And a mane that begins on the crown of its head and resembles horse hair, falls over its forehead covering its face, which makes it more terrifying when one meets it.

And it feeds upon poisonous roots. When it glares like a bull it immediately shudders and raises its mane, and when this has risen erect and the lips about its mouth are bared, it emits from its throat pungent and foul.

The Catoblepon or Gnu smelling (breath), so that the whole air overhead is infected, and any animals that approach and inhale it are grievously afflicted, lose their voice, and are seized with fatal convulsions. This beast is conscious of its power; and other animals know it too and flee from it as far away as they can.

7. The Elephant when hunted

Those who are adept at hunting Elephants constantly tell us that when these beasts are pursued they dash forward and are carried along with irresistible force and an impetus that nothing can withstand; there is no stopping them; they even rush through the largest trees as though they were standing corn, smashing the trees like cornstalks.

In one place the trees overtop them and hold their leaves above them, in another they themselves are higher than the trees. Indeed they run with all their might and baffle their pursuers by the course they take; which is natural, for they are familiar with the country.

And when they have got far away and are at a great distance ahead of the pursuing horsemen and have regained their courage through being secure from danger and feeling free, they pause and rest and are most glad to lay aside their anxious fears.

And then at this time they bethink them of food. They feed, so I hear, on the bushy mastic that grows around the trees and the wild ivy that creeps with its dense foliage over them, also upon the young and tender leaves of the date-palm and upon the more sappy shoots and twigs of other plants.

But if their pursuers again approach, the Elephants once more take to flight. And so when evening has overtaken them the pursuers bivouac, and by setting fire to the forest to some extent cut off the Elephants retreat and so bring them to a standstill. For Elephants no less than lions have a horror of fire.

8. Birds as Weather prophets

I learn from Aristotle that cranes flying in to land from the sea indicate to the intelligent man that a violent storm is threatening. But if the same birds are flying tranquilly, that is a promise of fine weather and a calm atmosphere; and if they make no sound they are reminding those who have experience that it will be fairly calm.

And if they (fly in from the sea?) uttering their cries and confusing their order in their agitation, there again they are threatening a heavy storm. And if a shearwater utters its cry at dusk, it apparently signifies the same; if it flies straight to the sea, it is giving a hint that a rainstorm will burst from the sky. If however the weather is stormy, the hooting of an owl portends fair weather and a bright day; whereas if the weather is fair and the owl hoots softly, you must expect storms. If a raven croaks volubly and peeks and shakes its wings, it is the first to observe that a storm is coming.

Again, if the raven, the crow, and the jackdaw utter their cries in the late afternoon, they teach us that we shall have a visitation by a storm. And if jackdaws, as the same writer says scream like hawks and fly now high now low, they point to frost and rain. If a crow caws softly at supper-time, it is inviting us to expect fair weather next day.

If birds appear in great numbers and they are white, it is a certain indication that there will be heavy storms. When ducks and shearwaters flap their wings, they point to violent winds. And when birds come speeding into land from the sea, this is evidence of stormy weather.

If the robin comes to cattle-sheds and houses, he is clearly trying to escape from a coming storm. Cockerels too and domestic fowls, when they flap their wings and step proudly and cluck, signify stormy weather.

When birds bathe, it is a sign that Wind is threatening, and it points to gusty weather. If during a storm bird's fly towards one another and in and out, it is a sign of fine weather. When birds congregate about meres and on river banks, they know that a storm is coming.

On the other hand when birds of the sea and lake come in to land, they know that there will be a heavy storm, whereas land birds hastening to moist places are heralds of fine weather, if, that is, they make no sound.

9. Animals as weather prophets

I have heard that the Egyptians assert that the antelope is the first creature to know when the Dog-star rises, and testifies to the fact by sneezing. The Libyans are equally bold in stoutly maintaining that in their country the goats also know in advance; they also give clear signs of impending rain.

For when they emerge from their pens they rush at full speed to their fodder. Later, when satisfied, they turn towards home, and facing in that direction remain still and wait for the herdsman to gather them in as quickly as possible.

And Hipparchus in the reign of Hiero the Tyrant was sitting in the theatre wearing a leathern jerkin, and astonished people by knowing in advance out of the clear weather then prevalent that a storm was coming.

And Hiero in his admiration of the man congratulated the people of Nicaea in Bithynia on having Hipparchus as a citizen. And when at Olympia Anaxagoras, likewise clad in a leathern jerkin, was watching the Olympic Games and a storm of rain burst, all Hellas sang his praises, and claimed that his wisdom was more that of a god than of a man.

And few if any are surprised that an ox, if rain threatens, lies down on his right side, contrariwise if fair weather is coming, on his left. And I have also heard the following facts which are calculated to astonish one.

If an ox bellows and sniffs the air, rain is inevitable. And if oxen eat copiously and more than is their custom, it portends a storm. When sheep dig the ground with their hoofs, it is likely to mean a storm; and if the rams mount them early in the day, it promises an early storm; and the same when goats lie huddled together.

When pigs appear in corn land, they inform us that the rain is departing. Now when lambs and kids leap on one another and frisk about, they promise a bright day. But when martens squeak and mice likewise, they are conjecturing that there will be a violent storm.

When Wolves quit lonely places and make straight for inhabited districts, they show thereby that they dread the onslaught of a coming storm. If a lion visits corn lands, it presages a drought. And if beasts of burden gambol and low more than is their custom; it shows that storm and rain are on their way; and if besides, they toss up the dust with their hoofs, it signifies the same.

If hares are seen in great numbers in the same places, it signifies fair weather, in all these matters men falls behind: they only know these changes when they occur.

10. The Hawk in Egypt

Here are further facts which I have heard touching Hawks. The ministers of Apollo in Egypt say that there are certain men called hawk- keepers for this reason: they feed and tend the Hawks belonging to the god.

Now the whole race of Hawks is consecrated to this god, but there are certain sacred birds which are fed upon carefully prepared food and which seem in nowise to differ from offerings made to the god. Now the men who have been charged with the care of these birds tell the uninformed that each of them (they are tended in a The Hawk in Egypt sacred grove) lays eggs in its nest.

They have, it is true, and the cares of all Hawks, but these sacred ones are their special charge. They take out the brains of birds which have been caught and throw them to the newly born Hawks: soft food for tender chicks.

But to those that are full-grown the keepers serve flesh and sinews, which furnish strengthening nourishment for birds of prey. Those however that are in the intermediate stage between chicks and full-grown birds are served with the hearts} and one may see the remains of them.

So the aforesaid difference of foods concedes the point that Hawks know what is appropriate and agreeable to each age; and they are particular about it and would never touch food unsuited to their age. At a certain season quails visit their country and other birds arrive in flocks and these sacred Hawks feast on them also.

11. The Dog's devotion to its master: Galba's dog

The following story, I think, also affords evidence of the unbreakable affection which Dogs have for those who keep them. In one of the civil wars at Rome when Galba the Roman was murdered, there was not one of the man's enemies that was able to cut off his head.

Although countless numbers competed for this trophy, until they had killed the Hound at his side that had been reared under his care and that maintained its affection with the utmost loyalty and fought on behalf of its dead master, as though it were a fellow soldier, sharer of the same tent, and friend to the very last. It is worth knowing what a deed was this, wrought not by a man I declare, but by a faithful Hound of valiant spirit.

Pyrrhus of Epirus was on a journey when he came upon the corpse of a man, who had been killed, with his Dog standing beside and guarding its master to prevent anybody from adding outrage to murder.

Now it happened that this was the third day for which the Dog was keeping its assiduous and most patient watch, unfed. And so when Pyrrhus learnt this he took pity on the dead man and ordered him to be buried; but as for the Dog, he directed that it should be cared for and gave it whatever one offers a dog with 0ne's hand, in sufficient quantity and of a nature to induce it to be friendly and well-disposed towards him; and little by little Pyrrhus drew the Dog away.

So much then for that. Now not so long after, there was a review of the hoplites, and the King whom I, mentioned above was looking on, and that same Dog was at his side. For most of the time it remained silent and completely gentle.

But directly it saw the murderers of its master in the review, it could not contain itself or remain where it was, but leaped upon them, barking and tearing them with its claws, and by frequently turning towards Pyrrhus did its best to make him see that it had caught the murderers.

And so a suspicion dawned upon the King and those about him, and the way in which the Dog barked at the aforesaid men caused them to reflect. The men were seized and put on the rack and confessed their crime.

To those who trample upon the ordinance of Zeus the god of fellowship and of affection and betray their friends in life and after death, all this seems a mere tale. But for my part I do not follow those who fail to appreciate the excellence of Nature which, if she has given brutes a share of kindliness and affection, has certainly given a larger share to us rational beings.

But they make no use of her gift. And what need is there to add to my story all the other crimes which men have committed against their friends for the sake of base gain, hatching plots and acting the traitor? It fills me with pain that a Dog should be shown to have more loyalty, more kindly feeling than man.

12. Octopus and Eagle

Here is another story which has come to my ears: it is about the Octopus. There was a rock rising from the sea, though not to a great height.

Now once upon a time an Octopus crawled up it and spread out its tentacles and was glad to warm itself (the weather was inclined to be stormy), though it did not at once assume the colour of the rock.

Octopuses do this naturally, to protect themselves against those who have designs upon them, and also that they themselves may ambush fishes. Now an Eagle, quick to mark its prey (though it got no good thereby), swooped with all the force of its wings upon the Octopus, reckoning to secure a ready meal for itself and its young.

But the creature's tentacles wreathed themselves round the Eagle, and clinging fast to its hated enemy dragged it down, and it was Octopus and Eagle a case of the hungry Wolf, as you might say.

And presently the Eagle was floating dead upon the sea for the sake of its meal. Birds in fact suffer countless misadventures of this kind, and men even more: for example. Cyrus the Second, the son of Cambyses among the Massagetae celebrated by Herodotus P0lycrates also who hastened to Oroetes with the intention of laying hands on his gold, and any who working for another's ill, wreaks ill for his own heart.

Brute beasts do not realise these dangers; human beings do, but fail to guard against them. What use to you, Cyrus and Polycrates, were a tongue, speech, teachers, and beatings? I say nothing of the others, for why should I give the most profitable advice to men who are deaf and senseless?

13. The Women of Paeonia

Let the women of Paeonia be proud: let them assume arrogant airs, since their conduct is celebrated. This is what they do: on their head they carry a vessel full of water, their neck held straight so that as they walk the vessel shall remain erect without upsetting.

They attach their children to their breast before suckling them; and fastening the rein of their husband's horse to one arm lead it to drink, while they use their hands to spin thread.

The Women of Paeonia was this that moved Darius to admiration when some young Paeonians, having equipped their sister in the manner described, brought her before him as he sat in judgment, in order that he might be attracted by such a concentration of self-help and show mercy to their country.

14. A pregnant Hound

And yet how far more impressive is Nature than the Paeonian women. A bitch was hunting; the quarry was a hare and the bitch was pregnant. As soon as she had attained the object of her pursuit, she left it to her master and drawing aside, dropped (so they say) nine puppies, which she then reared. And if the Women of Liguria pride themselves that they also after giving birth rise up and devote themselves to their household duties, they will, on hearing what the aforesaid bitch did, forgo their pride and hide their heads in shame.

Dog reveals sacrilege

Aristotle has told the story of the labor loving Mule and so has we earlier on, but the episode of the Dog, which also occurred in Athens, is not irrelevant.

A temple-thief who had waited for the midmost hour of night and had watched till men were deep asleep, came to the shrine of Asclepius and stole a number of offerings without, as he supposed, being seen.

There was however in the temple an excellent watcher, a Dog, more awake than the attendants, and it gave chase to the thief and never stopped barking, as with all its might it summoned others to witness what had been done. And so at first the thief and his companions in that crime pelted the Dog with stones; finally he dangled bread and cakes in front of it.

He had been careful to bring these things with him as an attraction to Dogs, as he supposed. Since however the Dog continued to bark when the thief came to the house where he lodged and when he came out again, it was discovered where the Dog belonged, while the inscriptions and the places where the offerings were set up lacked the missing objects.

The Athenians therefore concluded that this man was the thief, and by putting him on the rack discovered the whole affair. And the man was sentenced in accordance with the law, while the Dog was rewarded by being fed and cared for at the public expense for being a faithful watcher and second to none of the attendants in vigilance.

The Goat cures cataract

The Goat, it seems, is in fact skilful at curing that mist of the eyes which doctors call cataract, and it is even said that men have learnt this cure from the Goat. The method is as follows. When the Goat perceives that its sight has become clouded it goes to a bramble and applies its eye to a thorn. The thorn pricks it and the fluid is discharged, but the pupil remains unharmed and the Goat regains its sight without any need of man's skill and manipulation

15. Elephants their mutual devotion

Young Elephants cross a river by swimming, but the full-grown ones, if covered by the stream, raise their trunks above the Water, while the mother elephants carry their newly born young upon their tusks. It is the young who take the lead in danger and hardship; out of respect for their elders they give way to them in drinking and feeding, and they have no need at all of the laws of Lycurgus.

An Elephant old and weak or stricken with disease would never be abandoned by his fellows in the herd, but they stay beside him loyally and hasten to lend him strength on all occasions, especially when they are being pursued; and they fight on his behalf and through staying by him receive wounds, when they could escape.

The females would never desert the young they have borne, but they too remain loyally at their side even though hunters press hard upon them, and they would sooner relinquish their life than their offspring.

16. Laenilla and her sons

When I was a boy I knew an aged woman, Laenilla by name, and everybody used to point at her, and a story was told of her to this effect. My elders used to tell me that she had passionately loved a servant and used to sleep with him, thereby bringing a slur upon her own children.

They were well—born and belonged to the Senatorial order in Rome by descent from their fathers and remoter ancestors. Now the children for very shame were angry with their mother for her behavior and admonished her gently and spoke to her in private of the shamefulness of her conduct. But she, seething with lust and putting her love above her sons, accused them before the magistrate, alleging that they were plotting against him. The magistrate having a ready ear for calumny, and being of a suspicious and cowardly nature (those are attributes of an ignoble character), believed her. So her sons who had done no Wrong were put to death, while the Woman reaped the reward of her informing and slept freely with the slave.

O gods of our fathers, O Artemis of the childbed, and ye goddesses of birth, daughters of Hera, why, when we recall calamities that befell recently and in our own day, should we speak any more of Colchian Medea or Attic Procne?

17. Eagle and Tortoise

Eagles seize Tortoises and then dash them on rocks from a height, and having smashed the Tortoise's shell they extract and eat the flesh. It was in this way, I am told, that Aeschylus of Eleusis, the tragic poet, met his end.

Death of Aeschylus

Aeschylus was seated upon a rock, meditating, I suppose, and writing as usual. He had no hair on his head and was bald. Now an Eagle supposing his head to be a rock let the Tortoise which it was holding fall upon it. And the missile struck the aforesaid poet and killed him.

Ceryl and Halcyon

The Ceryl and the Halcyon feed side by side and live together. . . . And when the Ceryls are feeble with age the Halcyons place them on their back and carry them about upon their middle Wing- feathers, as they are called.

Women however look down upon those who are ageing, and cast their eyes on youths. And husbands are eager after girls and take no notice of their elderly legal wives: creatures gifted with speech are not ashamed to live more unreasonably than unreasoning animals.

The Raven

The Egyptians who live about the region called Coptus assert that no more than a pair of Ravens is seen there. And even those Romans who guard the mountain district because of the Emerald Mine, they also maintain that the same number of this species live there. And in that place there is a temple in honour of Apollo to whom, they say, the birds are sacred.

18. Animal peculiarities

Here again I may as well speak of the peculiarities of animals. The sheep and the ass seem inclined to be sluggish; fawns, roe-deer, gazelles, antelopes, hares (which poets style 'cowerers') are timorous creatures.

Timorous also are sparrows among birds, and the mullet among fishes. Baboons and goats are lecherous, and it is even said that the latter have intercourse with women a fact which Pindar appears to marvel at.

And even hounds are said to have assaulted women, and indeed it is reported that a woman in Rome was accused by her husband of adultery, and the adulterer in the case was stated to be a hound. And I have heard that baboons have fallen madly in love with girls and have even raped them, being more wanton than the little boys in the all-night revels of Menander.

The partridge is extremely lecherous and given to adultery; at any rate these birds are said to go after the hens stealthily and with hardly a sound. Dogs do not admit others to share their food on any account; at any rate they often tear one another over a bone, just like Menelaus and Paris over Helen.

I am told that the dogs of Memphis are the only ones that pool their prey and share their food. The hog is implacable and devoid of justice; at any rate these creatures eat one another's dead bodies.

And the majority of fishes do the same. But the most impious of all is the hippopotamus, for it even eats its own father. Flies and dogs are without shame and are not easily checked.

19. Hungry Wolves

Wolves are exceedingly fierce, and the Egyptians assert that they even eat one another, and that the way in which they plot against each other is, they say, as follows. They gather round in a circle and then start to run.

And when any of their number is overcome with dizziness from running round and round and collapses, the rest fall upon him as he lies, tear him to pieces, and eat him. They do this whenever their hunting is unsuccessful. For with them, provided they do nothing hungry, nothing else counts; just as with evil men nothing counts but money.

20. Monkey and baby

It seems that the Monkey is the most mischievous of animals; and even worse when it attempts to copy man.

For example, a Monkey observed from a distance a nurse washing a baby in a tub, observed how first of all she took off its swaddling clothes and then after the bath wrapped it up; it marked where she laid it to rest.

And when it saw the place unguarded, sprang in through an open window, from which it had a view of everything; took the baby from its cot; stripped it as it had chanced to see the nurse do; brought the tub out, and (there was water heating on some embers) poured boiling water over the wretched baby and even caused it to die most miserably.

21. The Hyena

It seems that the Hyena also and the Coro cottas, as they call it, are viciously clever animals. At any rate the Hyena prowls about cattle-folds by night and imitates men vomiting. And at the sound dogs come up, thinking it is a man. Where upon it seizes and devours them.

The 'Corocottas'

I shall now relate the villainy of the Coro cottas, of which I have actually heard. It conceals itself in thickets and then listens to woodcutters calling one another by name, and even to anything they say.

And then it imitates their voices and speaks (though the story may be fabulous) with a voice that sounds human at any rate, calling out the name which it has heard. And the man who has been called approaches: the animal withdraws and calls again: the man follows the voice all the more.

But when it has drawn him away from his fellow-workers and has got him alone, it seizes him and kills him and then makes a meal off him after luring him on with its call.

22. A Lion's vengeance

The Lion knows how to take vengeance on one who has
previously done him an injury, and even though the
vengeance be not immediate,' Yet doth he keep his anger
thereafter in his bosom, until he accomplish it' And Juba of
Mauretania, the father of the boy who was a hostage at Rome,
bears witness to this.

He was marching once through the desert against some tribes
who had revolted, when one of the youths who ran beside
him, well-born, handsome, and already fond of the chase,
struck with a javelin a Lion that chanced to appear by the
roadside : he hit the mark and wounded the beast, but failed
to kill it.

But the expedition was in haste; the animal drew off, and the
boy who had wounded it hurried by with the rest. Now when
a whole year had passed and Juba had accomplished his
purpose, returning by the same way he arrived at the spot
where the Lion had happened to be wounded.

And in spite of the multitude of men that same Lion came forward and, without touching anyone else, seized him who a year ago had wounded it, and pouring forth the gathered anger which it had been nursing all that while, tore to pieces the boy whom it had recognized.

But not a soul took vengeance: they were afraid of the fierce and absolutely terrifying anger of the Lion. And besides, their journey made them hasten.

23. The Crab: various species

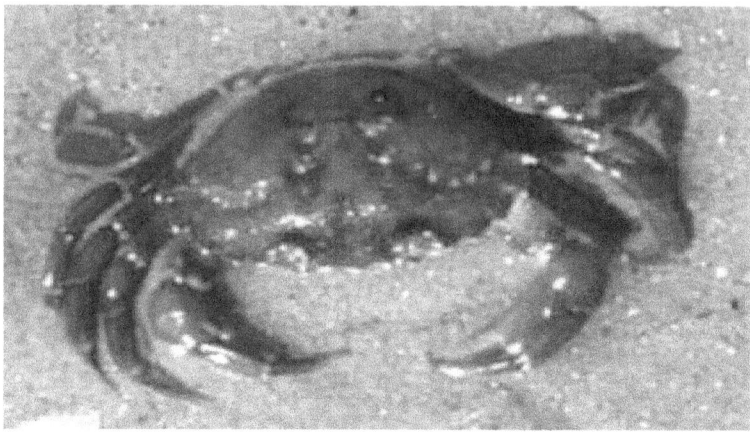

I have heard that there are different species and various tribes of Crabs, for there are some that live on rocks, but there are others besides, which mud, seaweed, and sand generate. And they have many shapes and many names.

And the Runner—crabs as they are called (and most appropriately) roam hither and thither, for it is neither their wish nor their nature to remain quiet and at rest in the same place, but they wander about the beaches where they were born; and they do in fact go further a field, just as human beings who are fond of travel.

The occasion of their wandering so far is their desire for more food of some kind. Now in the Thracian Bosphorus whenever the current comes down strongly from the Euxine, the Crabs wish to force their way upstream, but, as is natural, the stream breaks with too great violence round the headlands, so that if they should want to go against it, it will altogether thrust them back and defeat them.

Now the Crabs are already aware of this, and whenever they come near a headland each one halts in some bay-like spot and waits for the others. Then when they have congregated in one spot, they crawl up on to the land and scramble up on to the cliffs and so pass by on foot that part of the sea where the current is strongest.

Then having surmounted and passed the promontory, they descend once more to the sea. But the fishermen spare them because it is of their own free will that the Crabs crawl out on to the land: the men wish also to be spared themselves: they cannot bear to appear more cruel than the waves. live on rocks, but there are others besides, which mud, seaweed, and sand generate. And they have many shapes and many names. And the Runner-crabs as they are called (and most appropriately) roam hither and thither, for it is neither their wish nor their nature to remain quiet and at rest in the same place, but they wander about the beaches where they were born; and they do in fact go further a field, just as human beings who are fond of travel.

The occasion of their wandering so far is their desire for more food of some kind. Now in the Thracian Bosphorus whenever the current comes down strongly from the Euxine, the Crabs wish to force their way upstream, but, as is natural, the stream breaks with too great violence round the headlands, so that if they should want to go against it, it will altogether thrust them back and defeat them.

Now the Crabs are already aware of this, and whenever they come near a headland each one halts in some bay — like spot and waits for the others. Then when they have congregated in one spot, they crawl up on to the land and scramble up on to the cliffs and so pass by on foot that part of the sea where the current is strongest.

Then having surmounted and passed the promontory, they descend once more to the sea. But the fishermen spare them because it is of their own free will that the Crabs crawl out on to the land: the men wish also to be spared themselves: they cannot bear to appear more cruel than the waves.

24. Lap-dog and adulterer

I know that I have somewhere earlier on spoken of jealousy on the part of an animal not only extremely prudent but also extremely continent: it was, if my memory is sound, the Purple Coot. And I have now heard of a Lap-dog in Sicily that was the enemy of adulterers and a bitter foe to all of that class. The adulterer had concealed himself indoors, the lecherous woman having heard that her husband was returning from a journey; and the man was, as he supposed, well-situated for a hiding-place: for the servants, or those who were in league with their mistress to conceal the crime (there were 'such as were stewards of mirrors and of perfumes,' as Euripides and the doorkeepers too had been bribed, and this made the adulterer bold.

However matters did not turn out as intended; far from it. For the Lap-dog kept barking and even scratching with its paws at the door in such a way as , to alarm the master and to cause him by its action to guess that there was some mischief lurking. So naturally enough he threw open the door and caught the adulterer.

The man had a sword and was waiting till night fell so that he might kill the master of the house and thereupon marry the aforesaid woman.

25. The Goat and human spittle

Here is another example of the cleverness of Goats. They know full well that human spittle is deadly to other animals and they keep away from it, just as we also try to avoid anything that would injure a man were he to taste of it. Indeed it has happened before now that a man has in his ignorance and unconsciously swallowed some poison; but as to Goats, the aforesaid spittle would never take them unawares. And doubtless the same spittle is most effective at killing even sea-scolopendra.

A Goat that is destined for slaughter is well aware of it: witness the fact that it will no longer touch food. And a Goat disdains to bring up the rear of a flock of sheep, but must take the lead, and pro- claims it by its gait.

At any rate she walks ahead of them and the He-goat of the She-goats as well: his beard gives him confidence, and by some mysterious natural instinct he sets the male above the female.

Get All The Books In The Series:

Animal Peculiarity Volume 1 [1-8]
Animal Peculiarity Volume 2 [1-8]

www.ingramcontent.com/pod-product-compliance
Lightning Source LLC
Chambersburg PA
CBHW070348290526
45791CB00003B/1488